Arthur Penrhyn Stanley

The national thanksgiving

Sermons preached in Westminster abbey

Arthur Penrhyn Stanley

The national thanksgiving
Sermons preached in Westminster abbey

ISBN/EAN: 9783337104771

Printed in Europe, USA, Canada, Australia, Japan

Cover: Foto ©Lupo / pixelio.de

More available books at **www.hansebooks.com**

SERMONS

PREACHED IN WESTMINSTER ABBEY

The proceeds will be devoted to the Fund for the Restoration of St. Paul's Cathedral.

THE

NATIONAL THANKSGIVING

Sermons

PREACHED IN WESTMINSTER ABBEY

BY

ARTHUR PENRHYN STANLEY, D.D.

DEAN OF WESTMINSTER

London

MACMILLAN AND CO.

1872

LONDON : PRINTED BY
SPOTTISWOODE AND CO., NEW-STREET SQUARE
AND PARLIAMENT STREET

PREFACE.

It has been thought desirable to leave
on record some of the more permanent
thoughts connected with the successive
stages of the remarkable crisis through
which our country has passed during the
last three months. Many other discourses
may have expressed more directly the
individual feelings of the preacher. In
a large, mixed congregation, like that assembled in Westminster Abbey, it seemed
more fitting to speak of the general topics
which would remain after the immediate
occasion had passed, but which from this
occasion derived a force that could not
otherwise have been attained. A discourse
like that delivered by the Bishop of St.

David's on 'Christian Loyalty' * is an example of this use of the events of the time. It is hoped that these sermons may, under other aspects, recall, at least in some degree, the serious reflections which, if the nation is true to itself, ought not to perish with the moment.

* *Christian Loyalty.* A Sermon preached at St. Peter's, Carmarthen, on Sunday, January 21, 1872, by Connop Thirlwall, D.D., Bishop of St. David's.

CONTENTS.

I.

DEATH AND LIFE.

B

PREACHED IN WESTMINSTER ABBEY,

DECEMBER 10, 1871.

SERMON I.

PHIL. i. 21.

' To live is Christ, and to die is gain.'

ON a day like this—when there is one topic in
every household, one question on every lip—it
is impossible to stand in this place and not
endeavour to give some expression to that of
which every heart is full. By a natural Christian instinct, the whole nation is gathered into
one focus. We all press, as it were, round one
darkened chamber, we all feel that with the
mourning family, mother, wife, brothers, sisters,
who are there assembled, we are indeed one.
The thrill of their fears or hopes passes through
and through the differences of rank and station;
we feel that, whilst they represent the whole
people, they also represent and are that which
each family, and each member of each family,
is separately. In the fierce battle between Life

and Death, for the issues of which we are all
looking with such eager expectation, we see the
likeness of what will befall every individual
soul amongst us; and the reflection which this
struggle, with all its manifold uncertainties, sug-
gests, concerns us all alike.

I have thought, therefore, that it is best to fix
our minds for a few moments on what that
struggle involves—to ask what are the true
lessons of Life and of Death; to ask why it is
that, whether as men, or citizens, or Christians,
we desire with such prolonged earnestness that
Life, and not Death, may be the issue of this
mortal agony.

In doing so, let us be guided by the words
of St. Paul. He is writing to his best-beloved
converts. He opens his heart more fully to
them than to any others. He admits them, as
though they were his own brothers and friends,
to his innermost chamber. He discloses to
them his doubts, his anxieties, his weaknesses.
He describes to them the danger in which he
is—danger, we know not whether of natural

sickness or of a violent end. He looks on
Death and he looks on Life, and he knows not
which to choose; he sees the good of each. At
last he decides that what might have seemed
the best for him is not really the best; that
what might have seemed the worst for him is
not really the worst. He tells us, in short,
what are the reasons for desiring Death; but
he tells us still more strongly what are the
reasons for desiring Life.

It may seem almost cold thus to balance and
weigh the searchings of the heart at such moments. Yet it was not coldness in the Apostle;
it was the depth of tenderness. It is not coldness in us; it is the only channel into which we
can profitably turn our thoughts on such an
occasion, and make it yield its proper lesson.

I have, before this, in quite another connec-
tion, used these words of the Apostle. I know
not how to do better than to use them again to-
day, sharpened and pointed as they are by the
feelings of the moment, even to 'the dividing
'asunder of soul and spirit, and discerning even

'the thoughts and intents' of our innermost hearts.

To die is gain. Who is there that has not from time to time felt this, as he looks at the sufferings of this mortal life ; as he thinks of the wearing nights and days of sickness, of the restlessness, the sinking, the pain, the despair, the distress of the watchers, the prolonged agony of the bystanders ; as he looks at the miseries of this sinful world—the disappointments of brilliant hopes, the sore temptations to evil, the multiplied chances of failure ? Who, as he thus thinks of himself or of others, has not been moved to say, from time to time, 'Oh that I had the wings of a dove, that I 'might flee far away and be at rest!' It is the feeling beautifully expressed by the greatest of our poets, when he says :—

> Tired with all these, for restful death I cry,—
> As, to behold desert, a beggar born,
> And needy nothing trimm'd in jollity,
> And purest faith unhappily forsworn,
> And gilded honour shamefully misplaced,
> And right perfection wrongfully disgraced,
> And art made tongue-tied by authority,

> And folly, doctor like, controlling skill,
>   And simple truth, miscall'd simplicity,
>   And captive Good attending Captain Ill :
>   Tired with all these, from these would I be gone.

So wrote Shakspeare in his famous sonnet, and so felt even the great Apostle when, amidst the desertion of friends, and the hard struggle of truth against falsehood and good against evil, he desired to be at rest and be with his Master beyond the grave, which, he says, 'would be far better.'

So, too, we for ourselves, and for those that we love, and for those whose lives are fraught with so many chances of fatal shipwreck, may well long for that day when we and they shall have shuffled off this mortal coil ; when we shall have done with the anxious trials, the paltry quarrels, the baffled hopes, the grinding toil of the great Babylon of this harassing world ; when we shall have escaped from the burden and heat of the day, from the roar and tumult of the swollen torrent of life, to be with those beloved departed,

> Who in the mountain grots of Eden lie,
> And hear the fourfold river as it murmurs by.

In this sense Death is, and must be, a gain to
all. And it is by reflecting on this clear gain
that the mind bows itself to the Supreme Will,
and the heart nerves itself to the terrible
thought of the last dread summons from all
that we see and love in this earthly scene. It is
for this that, in the language of our Visitation
Service, we commit the soul with such assured
confidence into the hands of its faithful Creator
and most merciful Saviour.

But the Apostle tells us that after all there
is something yet greater than the gain and rest
of Death, and that is the struggle and victory
of Life. Death was gain to him, but Life was
something more. '*To live is* CHRIST.' Death
in one sense is the gate of Life eternal ;
but Life—this mortal life—is the only true
gate of a happy and peaceful death. It is
in Life—in the wear and tear of Life—that
those graces must be wrought and fashioned
which perfect the soul, immortal over Death.
'Reckon yourselves,' says the Apostle, 'to be
'*dead to sin.*' But there is something much

more than this, 'Reckon yourselves *to be alive*
'to God through Christ.' He preaches with all
his heart and soul, not the worthlessness, but
the infinite preciousness of Life.

Those lines from our great poet, which I
quoted just now, describing his weariness of
the world, close with the one thought which
reconciled him to remaining :—

> Tired with all these, from these would I be gone,
> Save that, to die, I leave my love alone.

That, doubtless, is one chief thought that
makes earthly life dear to us—the thought
that it contains those whom our departure
would leave desolate and alone. But in fact
this sense of human love is a likeness, like all
pure earthly affections, of a feeling far higher.
When the heathen, when the unbeliever have
often sought escape from the troubles of life by
self-destruction, they have done so to escape
from that which to them had no sacred value.
But the Christian, the believer in God and in
Christ, has, or ought to have, the abiding con-
sciousness that in Life there are not only (it may

be) the dearest objects of his earthly affection, but that there is the very work, the very presence of Christ. It is one of the points of coincidence between true Christianity and true civilisation. As mankind advances in civilisation, human life becomes more sacred, more precious ; as mankind advances in Christianity, the human soul, which is but another word for human life, becomes more precious, more sacred also. By leaving our work here before the time, we should leave His work undone. By turning our backs in self-will or impatience on this mortal scene, we should be turning our backs on Him who is in those very sufferings and struggles most surely to be found.

Every kindness done to others in our daily walk, every attempt to make others happy, every prejudice overcome, every truth more clearly perceived, every difficulty subdued, every sin left behind, every temptation trampled under foot, every step forward in the cause of good, is a step nearer to the life of Christ, through which only death can be really a gain to us. Death may be great, but Life is greater still. Death may be a state to be desired for ourselves, rejoiced in for others, but Life is the state in which Christ makes Himself known to us, and through which we must make ourselves known to Him. He sanctified and glorified every stage of it. He was a little child, and showed us how good it was to be obedient to our parents—how dear to a mother a child could be—how He never forgot her, but even on the cross thought of what would soothe and comfort her. He grew up to boyhood—he showed us how to learn, both by hearing and asking questions—how early He could be busied in doing His Father's work. He showed us in full manhood how, in the midst of the world, and of constant pressing duties—many coming and going—in feasting and in company, no less than in serious moments, He still was the same Divine Master and Friend. He showed us in the desolation and solitude of Gethsemane and Calvary, when He seemed to be left, unsupported,

to Himself, that He was yet not alone, because
the Father was with Him. This is the way
in which this poor human life may become a
Divine life, may become a life of Christ.

Therefore, when we apply these words and
thoughts to ourselves, what is it but to dwell not
on the misuse, but on the use of our existence?
Think how much yet remains to be done in the
thirty, twenty—yes, even in the ten years, or
perhaps in the one year, perhaps even in the
one day, that yet may remain to us. Despise
it not, neglect it not ; cherish, enlarge, improve
this vast, this inestimable gift, whilst it is
granted to us with its endless opportunities,
with its boundless capacities, with its glorious
hopes, with its indispensable calls, with its im-
mense results, with its rare chances of repent-
ance, of improvement, even for the humblest
and weakest among us.

To rise above ourselves, to lose ourselves in
the thought of the work, great or small, that
God has placed before us—to live in that life
which is indeed eternal, because it belongs both

to this world and the next—for the sake of
doing this the Apostle could consent to live,
could prefer life with all its sorrows to death
with all its gain. 'God is not a God of the
'dead, but of the living.' Christ is not a dead
Christ, but a living Christ. 'The living, the
'living, he shall praise Thee, he shall serve
'Thee.' The varied duties of common life—the
daily round, the trivial task—are the means by
which we carry on the true Apostolical succession of Christ's first servants. 'There may be
'everywhere'—I quote the words of a devoted
Christian of another country—'there may be
'everywhere a silent apostleship, a persuasive
'and incessant sermon—namely, the natural
'brightness of a profound and true content.
'Never can the immortal hopes to which our de-
'votion renders its sacrifice be so well proclaimed
'by our words, as by the radiant tranquillity of
'that inward repose which comes up from the
'heart to the countenance.' 'I find'—so said this
same saint-like person—'I find Death perfectly
'desirable, but I find Life perfectly beautiful.'

And what is true of the life of individuals
is true also of the life of great communities.
There is, indeed, both of individuals and of
nations, a life which is not a life, empty, dead, bar-
ren, a mere existence, vanity of vanities. But the
collective life of thousands of English Christian
souls—the life of the heart of a great people—
life, not stagnation, life, not idleness—is the very
element, the living element in which the spirit
of man lives and makes others live—of which
the Spirit of Christ, which is Christ Himself,
is the life and the light. This is what is meant
by saying that the Church—that is the Christian society, the living company of all good men,
the souls and hearts of Christian men and women—forms 'the Body' of Christ. We, whether
singly or collectively, are His representatives—
we are (so the Bible repeatedly tells us) His
very self. In all that is best and purest in us, in
our duties, in our hopes, He lives. Because He
lives we live. Because we live He lives. It is
sometimes asked—it was asked the other day by
an eloquent preacher in the great neighbouring

Cathedral—whether the Christ, the Historical
Person who lived eighteen hundred years ago,
is still alive amongst us. It is also sometimes
asked, in many forms, and with many forms
of reply, how and where Christ's presence is to
be found and felt. But the best answer to all
these questions is the answer of the Apostle,
'To live is Christ.' It is so, as I have said, on
the smallest scale in our individual existence. It
is so on the largest scale. 'The Life of Chris-
'tendom is the Life of Christ.' That is the proof,
the evidence, the direct continuation of the
life of Christ. It is through the multitudinous
mass of living human hearts, of human acts
and words of love and truth, that the CHRIST
of the first century becomes the CHRIST of the
nineteenth. Each successive age, each separate nation, does His work on a larger and still
larger scale. The arts, the literature, the sciences,
the charities, the liberties, the laws, the worship of the commonwealths of Christian Europe
are all parts of the living body of CHRIST.
Their influence on us is part of His influence.

Their benefits to us are part of 'the innumerable 'benefits of His Cross and Passion.' To live under the best influences of Christendom, to live under the best influences of Christian England, this for us, and this only, is—the Apostle allows us to say so—is CHRIST Himself.

And now, O my brethren, if there be an individual life to which much that I have already said be applicable—a life dear to hundreds of loving friends, and to a most loving family—a life which in their service and affection finds its best inspirations and its best vitality—a life which had till now (humanly speaking) long years of usefulness and happiness before it ; then for the preservation of that life, for the sake of him who now lies on the dark confines of hope and fear, and for the sake of those most near and dear to him, we may and must earnestly pray and trust that it may by God's blessing be preserved. And when we add the further thought that this is a life which may, if so be, influence to an untold degree the national existence of which I just now spoke—a life which, if duly appreciated and

fitly used, contains within it special opportunities of good such as no other existence in this
great community possesses—a life which may,
if worthily employed, stimulate all that is noble
and beneficent, and discourage all that is low and
base and frivolous—which, from its exceptional
position, will have the power of moderating the
extremes of party zeal, and of pursuing the
common weal of all with an energy not weak-
ened or divided by local or partial claims—a life
which, if spared, may be the instrument for
making us more and more to be of one mind
and heart in all that is just and good, even as
at this moment the fear of losing it has brought
us all together with one heart and one soul.
Such a life is worth living, is worth praying for,
and for such a life, for such a Royal life—which
is so dear now to those who watch its fluctu-
ations from hour to hour beside and around the
bed of sickness—which may, with God's blessing, be so precious for our children and our
children's children—we pray that it may yet be

prolonged for the good of men and the glory
of God, through Jesus Christ, our Lord, who is
'the Resurrection and the Life, in whom whose-
'ever believeth, though he were dead yet shall
'he live.'

II.

THE

TRUMPET OF PATMOS.

PREACHED IN WESTMINSTER ABBEY,

DECEMBER 17, 1871.

SERMON II.

REV. i. 10.

*' I was in the Spirit on the Lord's day, and heard
behind me a great voice, as of a trumpet.'*

THE new Calendar of Lessons, which has been
followed for some months in this church, intro-
duces for the first time in the Services of this
Sunday portions from the Book of the Revelation of St. John. The history of the reception
of that book in the Church is curious and
instructive. For the first three centuries it was
not regularly received amongst the Canonical
Books of Scripture, and even after it was received—even at the time of the Reformation—
very few lessons were selected from it to be read
in public. The reasons for this are obvious. The
Book is in fact exceedingly obscure—and it has
been made even more obscure by the fancies
of interpreters. It was also in ancient times

looked upon askance, because it was the favourite
text-book of those who were then thought here-
tics, and in modern times because it has been
the favourite text-book of angry polemics and
fanciful diviners of the future — the source
whence have been drawn weapons of offence
against theological adversaries, or imaginary
pictures of the history of modern Europe. But
in spite of these objections, it has, by the force
of its sublime poetic form and its high moral
tone, held its ground, and the true instinct of
Christendom has been shown in the fact, that
without the sanction of Councils and against
the opinion of great prelates, this mysterious
book has gradually forced its way into the Canon
of Scripture, and now at last, after having been
almost excluded from the public service of the
English Church, it has been appointed to be read
during the last month in the year, when its
lessons naturally fall in with the season of Ad-
vent. Some chapters are still omitted, as fit
rather for the solitary student than for the
mixed congregation. But there is enough given

to express the general tenor of the book, and it is of this general tenor that I propose to speak, and of this with its special application to ourselves.

The Prophet (for as such we must regard the author of this sacred book) was on the solitary island of Patmos, withdrawn from earthly things, like Moses on Sinai, or Elijah on Carmel. Round about him was the bright Ægean Sea, with its hundred isles and the neighbouring mountains of Asia Minor, within whose circle lay the familiar Seven Churches to which his epistles and addresses were sent.* And it was on the Lord's day. He was wrapt in the stillness and devotion of the day, already even in that early time set apart for the contemplation of heavenly things. Such was the external framework of the prophecy. It was in this solitude, in this solemn scene, from this lonely peak of speculation, that there was unrolled before the eye of his spirit that vision of the future which is called the 'Apocalypse,' that is the 'Revela-

---

* See Appendix to *Sermons in the East*, pp. 225-231.

tion,' the 'Unveiling' of the will and purpose
of Providence.

Amidst all that is obscure and difficult, there
are two main features of this Revelation which
may be easily described and easily understood.
The first is that, as in all the prophetic visions of
the Bible, the outward imagery is taken from the
objects and circumstances immediately at hand
and around. Not only do the bright sky, the
wide sea, the lofty mountains, the grotesque
rocks, the sandy beach, of Patmos and the ad-
jacent islands enter into the picture, but the
whole tissue of the visions themselves is drawn
from the events with which the atmosphere of
that portentous time was charged. It was the
period which witnessed the fulfilment of those
signs in earth and heaven which are set forth
in the Gospel records brought before us at this
season. The long peace which had prevailed
throughout the world down to the death of the
Emperor Nero had just been broken up. It
was the epoch which the Roman historian describes as 'teeming with disasters, terrible in

' war, rent with faction, savage even in peace.
From the Northern Ocean to the Ægean coasts,
all was in confusion and alarm — wars and
rumours of wars, earthquakes, volcanoes, armies
marching and countermarching, the fall of
Jerusalem, the burning of Rome, the overthrow
of the cities of Herculaneum and Pompeii, the
barbarians hanging on the frontier, dynasty
after dynasty succeeding each other on the
imperial throne, ' the powers of heaven shaken,
' men's hearts failing them for fear of those
' things that were coming on the earth.' This
was the horizon on which the Prophet looked
out, and it was the thought of these calamities
which presented to him the imagery of those
prophecies which have themselves continued the
like imagery for all such convulsions in every
age. The ' thunderings and lightnings and
' earthquakes,' ' the trumpets of war ' and ' the
' vials of wrath,' the overthrow of the Imperial
city on her seven hills, the bottomless pit, and
Death on his pale horse, all these are the signs
which he read in the lowering heavens and the

distracted earth of his own times. And on the
other hand, the martyrs under the throne, the
white-robed army of saints, the new Jerusalem
coming down as a bride adorned for her hus-
band, were suggested by the thought of the
little band of Christians already spreading
through the Empire, already becoming the
centres of light and life and truth amidst a
corrupt, decaying, and dissolving world; struggling against their fanatical persecutors in the
Jewish Church, and their heathen persecutors
in the Roman Empire, yet still holding their
own, and containing within themselves the
pledge of the future of civilisation and of
Christianity. It is needless, it is futile to seek
in these chapters for the detailed history of our
own recent times. They have no relation to
modern events; they belong, as far as their
letter is concerned, to the States and the
Churches which formed the horizon, far or near,
of the Seer on the rock of Patmos, in the first
century of the Christian era—not to the States
and Churches of Italy, France, Germany, or

England, in the sixteenth, or eighteenth, or nineteenth, or twentieth centuries, as some in all succeeding generations have vainly tried to find them.

There is much in them that we shall never understand—they are riddles of which the key is lost ; 'the times and the seasons that the 'Father has put in His own power,' and 'which 'are not known to the Angels of God, nor even 'to the Son of Man,' are not likely to be discovered by any process of interpretation, however ingenious, from this sacred book, which, as regards these outward things, was addressed to the generation not of some future age, but of that which its author was specially sent to waken and to warn.

But, secondly, there is an eternal truth wrapt up in these sublime visions—in their spirit, and not in their letter; in their general principles, not in their details. On that great Lord's day St. John was not in the flesh, not in the time or space of any particular scene or spot on earth, but 'in the Spirit.' And 'in the Spirit,' under

these outward forms, he described how through
struggles, through miseries and confusions of
every kind, the cause of goodness and truth, the
spiritual man (so to speak) of the whole human race advances towards perfection.   From
that solitary rock he saw the shaking of em-
pires, the ruin of nations, the persecution of the
saints, the blood of the martyrs; yet he felt
persuaded, and in his bright and beaming words
of hope and triumph, he has stamped on the
mind of Christendom his persuasion, that purity
and truth would come out victorious at last.
It is at times a hard doctrine to receive.   It
seems at times as if the advance of civilisation, of religion, of goodness were so irregular
that we almost despair of the ultimate purposes of Providence—of the final perfection of
humanity.   Yet the Seer of Patmos did not despair, nor was troubled beyond measure; and
so, neither should our hearts fail.

In the voice of the trumpet that spoke behind
him, however varied its tones, he recognised, and
we should recognise, the voice of God.   Even

when, as then, the progress of humanity seemed to be thrown back, and ancient superstitions seemed to be regaining their hold, he clung, and we may still cling, to the hope that good will be wrought out of evil ; even when we look on the grievous crimes and follies which have brought about the fall of nations, we may speak of them, as even in that hour of judgment St. John himself spoke of them, with a feeling of human sympathy for the wreck of imperial greatness and worldwide splendour.

These, then, are the two main features of the Apocalypse. First, the interest, which the public events of our own time are intended to awaken in the hearts of Christians. Secondly, the moral and spiritual effect which such an interest is intended to produce.

Other signs, other striking events, have occurred in the earlier part of this year on which I have before dwelt,* as like to those greater

---

* I refer to sermons preached in the earlier part of 1871, during the troubles of France and the conflagration of Paris.

convulsions of which the Revelation speaks. But it seems to me that we shall be also following out the spirit of this sacred book, if we fix our attention on the one public event, close at hand, which has recently filled our minds; if we concentrate our thoughts on that one single trumpet-call, and ask what permanent good we may learn from it.

We were all of us engaged in our several pursuits; most of us as much withdrawn from any of the concerns which were going on outside of our own immediate circles as St. John was removed from all thoughts of the great Roman Empire in his seclusion in the isle of Patmos. Suddenly, like him, we everyone of us were roused from these separate individual cares; everyone, however high or however humble, in the midst of our several distractions and occupations, as though we heard the voice of a trumpet talking with us. It came not from falling thrones, or blood-stained battle-fields, or burning cities, but from a single sick chamber in a secluded English county. At

each successive reverberation of that thrilling
voice, as it was repeated from city to city in
countless messages, it hushed the strife of angry
disputants, it silenced the eager gathering, it
broke up the festive banquet, it rang on from
shore to shore through the vast range of the
whole empire ; the whole nation of Englishmen
became on a sudden possessed with one thought
and one desire. Even the remote subjects of
our dominion, of other races and other creeds,
joined in one united prayer for one single youthful life, that it might be sustained in its fierce
struggle with death. And now that the tones of
that trumpet are changed from mourning into
joy, from despair into hope, not the less are its
vibrations felt in every household and in every
heart.

My brethren, there is not yet such absolute
confidence as that we can indulge in assured
thanksgiving for the answer to our hopes ;
and it is not till that day arrives that we can
look forward, as we then ought to look forward,
with solemn and serious thoughts to the fresh

duties which the gracious mercy of God will then, if so be, impose both on him who is spared, and on us who have so earnestly trusted that he might be spared.

But we may, even now, before the recollection of our strain of eager expectation and anxiety has faded away, ask ourselves what this voice was intended to teach us; we may seek to give the reasons to ourselves and to other nations why our hearts have thus burned within us—why, by the mortal struggle of a single existence, our souls were so deeply stirred.

There were many feelings which this unexpected trumpet-call awakened in us, that made it like a voice from a better world.

Let me speak of a few of these. I confine myself to those which apply to all of us alike.

The first lesson of such a summons is that it called us out of ourselves. Nothing is so narrowing, contracting, hardening, as always to be moving in the same groove, with no thought beyond what we immediately see and hear close around us. Any shock which breaks this even course, anything which makes us think of other joys and sorrows besides our own, is of itself chastening, sanctifying, edifying. We are, or ought to be, the better for having had our souls filled with the thought of others, whom many of us never saw, with hopes and fears which went far beyond the small span of our own lives into the distant future.

Secondly, it touched a chord which vibrates even in the least responsive hearts. It appealed to our sense of the sanctity, the preciousness of family ties; it drew us round one family hearth. In every condition of life a natural instinct prompted an instantaneous sympathy with and for the sufferer and those who were watching around him, because in every household the same scene might at any moment be enacted. It made us feel, according to the trite saying, that royal persons are of the same flesh and blood with us; but it also

D

made us feel—which is no less important—
that we are of the same flesh and blood with
them. That strain of suspense, that sorrow,
that joy which we all of us have felt, was a
testimony to the true nobleness and greatness
of home affections. Let us, as we think over
this week, thank God that He has planted these
instincts within us. Let no one be ashamed
to own, let everyone be eager to cherish, these
pure and sacred feelings, which a whole nation
has been proud to exhibit, and which are in
fact the foundation of all true national and
all true Christian life.

Thirdly, it has brought before us how,
amidst all our dissensions and party strifes,
we are still Englishmen—Englishmen, first
and foremost, whatever we may be besides.
This is not the first time that the like
penetrating sympathy with a single member
of the royal house has knit together the hearts
of all. So it was, as our fathers have told us,
when the Princess Charlotte was snatched
away in a moment of time with her infant

child. So it was on that sad day which, on its tenth anniversary in this past week, filled every mind with dark forebodings, when the illustrious Prince, whose loss is still felt throughout the Empire, was called away in the midst of his beneficent career. So it has been in that alternation of grief and hope which has wavered round the sick bed of the Heir of the remote future. This it is which gives to the Family that represents the whole people so rare, so singular an interest. It brings before us in a living, present shape the fact that above and beyond all sects and parties there is such a thing as an inextinguishable feeling towards our common country, a sacred bond in the thought that one familiar name calls up all our patriotic emotions, a charm which gilds the wear and tear of politics with a personal devotion, such as no mere abstraction could enkindle. I have often before and elsewhere dwelt on the sacredness of a Christian State, on the paramount supremacy of

the English Crown and the English Law. It
is impossible to imagine a more striking tribute
than that which has been just rendered to this
sometimes forgotten and disparaged truth, by
the spontaneous outburst of every class and
of every party. There are nations, and there
have been times in which the devotion to the
reigning family has been a thing separate and
apart from the love of country. There have
been times and places, where the love of
country has existed with no loyal feeling to
the reigning family. Let us thank God that
in England it is not so. Loyalty with us is the
personal, romantic side of Patriotism. Patriotism
with us is the Christian, philosophic side of
Loyalty. Long may the two flourish together,
each supporting and sustaining the other.

And, finally, this universal movement has
shown—what in the last resort Englishmen have
always shown—that we are (I say it not in any
spirit of boastfulness or ostentation) a Godfearing
and religious people. What was the natural expression of our hopes and fears—our sympathy

and the anxious expectation ? It was the united sacred language of prayer to the Supreme Ruler and Father of the Universe. Not only in the churches in which, as here, day after day, the names of the Sovereign and her children are habitually mentioned, and where, in silent meditation, each of those names has through the whole of this long suspense been commended to God, not only in the solemn prayer which on last Sunday was offered up with one consent in every proud cathedral and humble village church which owns the Queen's authority, but in every church and chapel of every sect, however far removed from our mode of worship or doctrine ; in temples of other faiths in regions far away ; in journals at home, however cynical and worldly ; in assemblies however secular, the same awful Name was invoked, the same devout wish was expressed, the same sacred petition breathed, differing in words, but in substance the same. This is indeed a true Christian communion ; this is to keep the unity of the spirit in the bond of peace. We need not penetrate into the inscrutable secrets of Providence—we need not perplex ourselves with precise questions on the mode in which Prayer is answered. It is enough for us to know and feel that it is the most natural, the most powerful, the most elevated expression of our thoughts and wishes in all great emergencies. It is enough to know that in the most severe of all trials, the most sustaining and comforting thought is the fixed belief that we are in the hands of an All-wise, All-merciful Father. To Him we turned in anxious suspense, to Him we turn again with grateful thanks. Into His Hands we commended the spirit of the sufferer, hovering between life and death, to be strengthened, purified, and, if it might so be, restored to us. Into those same Hands of infinite compassion we commend once more that same youthful spirit, returning, as we trust, from the gates of the grave to a higher, better, grander life than ever before.

May we be strengthened by the voice of the heavenly Trumpet to fulfil more faithfully, more loyally, more courageously our duty towards him; may he be strengthened by that same voice, as from another world, to fulfil more actively, more steadfastly, more zealously his duty towards us. ' Unto God's gracious mercy and protection we ' commit him. The Lord bless him and keep ' him. The Lord make His face to shine upon ' him, and be gracious unto him.'

III.

THE

DAY OF THANKSGIVING.

PREACHED IN WESTMINSTER ABBEY,

MARCH 3, 1872.

SERMON III.

PSALM cxxii. I.

'I was glad when they said unto me, We will go into the house of the Lord.'

THESE words, taken from the Psalms of the 27th day of the month, which I have caused to be again repeated here to-day, met the eyes of thousands in the course of the past week, inscribed over the western portico of St. Paul's Cathedral. They fitly expressed the feeling which swayed the heart of the whole metropolis. We were glad, we rejoiced, because our Sovereign and her people had said, 'We will go into the house of the Lord.' It was a gladness which made itself felt even to the distant extremities of our mighty Empire. It was a gladness for the gracious gift, as if sent direct from heaven, of a precious life which we had earnestly sought. It was the gladness of beholding the Sovereign whom we loved once more trusting herself amongst us, and receiving with radiant smiles, with unshaken courage, the tokens of her people's loyalty. It was the thankful gladness, we may say, for the Thanksgiving itself, the grateful relief, that a day so long expected with such eagerness, we had well nigh said with such awe, as its morning dawned with its mighty burden of innumerable human souls, had come and gone amidst such almost unclouded brightness, such almost unbroken order and pure unstained enjoyment.

But it was not mere gladness—not mere thanksgiving. When we felt that the centre of all those myriad movements was not the seat of commerce, or legislation, or pleasure, but the consecrated house of the Lord—when we looked down on the multitudes covering that vast area, or upwards to the multitudes suspended in that soaring cupola—when after the long hours of waiting, there fell over all those dense masses a stillness, as of an unseen

Presence—when, as the voice of praise and
prayer went up from thousands of lips and
thousands of hearts, the whole atmosphere
became, as it were, charged with worship—we
felt assured that the ages of faith are not yet run
out, that Religion, in its widest and deepest sense,
still holds its sway over the hearts of Englishmen, that it shall be, as far as human foresight
can reach, the crown and consummation and best
expression of our noblest and purest feelings.
And when further we remarked, how, under that
spacious dome were gathered (with the single
exception of one exclusive body), the representatives of every Christian, nay, of every religious
community in England, how all of these felt
that, agreeing here or disagreeing there, they
yet on the whole could join in the utterances
of religious faith and hope as embodied in
the venerable forms of the National Church—
it was a living proof that such united worship
within one common national sanctuary is not
an idle dream; it was a sign that a National
Church, so bound up, heart and soul, life and

limb, with the Nation and the State, could alone
furnish such a common meeting-point of religion
and patriotism—it was a pledge that as long as
the memory of that day remains, England will
not willingly consent to make over her noblest
historical and sacred edifices, her purest and
highest aspirations after God, to the keeping of
any single sect, or to the mere rivalry and con-
tention of private interests.

When further we thought how he who was the
central object of that vast gathering, was there
not merely as an ordinary worshipper, but as
one who had, by a marvellous recovery re-
turned from the very valley of the shadow of
death—and that, by a singular coincidence, the
Primate's words of sober and simple counsel
were uttered by one who had himself been
recalled by a recovery not less wonderful to
health and activity amongst us—a dying man,
speaking as to a dying man of the duties of the
living to which both had been alike brought back
—when we remember how around that youthful
form life and death had battled, for long days and

nights, like mortal combatants, in a strife of
which the whole English race were the awe-
struck spectators—when we glanced at the
mother, wife, brothers, sisters, and little children,
in whose anguish, and anxious expectation, and
returning happiness all the nation found the im-
personation of their own peculiar joys and sorrows—then, again, we felt that it was not merely
a solemn service, a sacred act of adoration,
but a service, a worship, of the most living
reality—because it rose from and gathered
round a living human being, with passions, hopes,
fears, duties, such as each one of us knows in
himself, needing the same strength from above,
struggling with the same terrible temptations,
wrought in the same English mould, inheritor
of the same individual destiny for weal or woe,
according to the deeds done in the body,
whether they be good or whether they be evil.
Other services might be more ornate, more
dramatic ; other appeals to the feelings more
exciting ; other forms of devotion more eager
to pry into the secrets of the eternal world, or

explain the unrevealed mysteries of Providence. We were content with the simple expression of heartfelt gratitude, as of sons to a Father, for a mercy received,—and if that natural expression rose to gigantic proportions, it was only because the whole nation was resolved to bear its part therein.

But yet more ; not only was this a solemn religious festival—not only did it concern the welfare of a human soul, which, whether of Prince or peasant, is equally precious in the sight of the Eternal God- ·but it was the response in every English heart to the sense of the union, too subtle for analysis, yet true and simple as the primitive instincts of our race—which binds the people of England to their monarchy, and the monarchy to the people. It is the feeling of which the Psalms are so noble a rendering, and which make them so fit an exponent of our national hopes and fears.— ' There is the seat of judgment. There are the ' thrones of the house of David. For my brethren ' and companions' sake, I will wish thee prosperity;

'yea, because of the House of the Lord our God,
'I will seek to do thee good.' So spoke the
Psalmist in the inspired thanksgiving, from
which the text is taken. And so in a yet more
exalted strain, another Psalmist drew a picture
of what such a monarchy should be —'Give thy
'judgments, O God, to the king, and thy right-
'eousness to the king's son. He shall judge thy
'people with righteousness, and thy poor with
'judgment. He shall deliver the needy when
'he crieth, and the poor also, and him that hath
'no helper. In his days shall the righteous
'flourish, and abundance of peace, so long as the
'moon endureth.'

Such was the ideal of a just and beneficent
Monarchy more than two thousand years ago.
Such, to all who can feel or think, it still is,
amidst whatever mixture of personal and national infirmity, amidst whatever changes have
been wrought by differences of time and race
and country, in our modern existence.

Look for a moment at the serious philosophic, Christian aspect of such a monarchy, as

that which alone rendered possible the feelings
of the week that is past.   It is the one name
and place amongst us which unites in almost
unbroken succession the whole range of our
island story, which is the common property of
the whole British people, we might almost say
of the whole Anglo-Saxon race.   No other
existing throne in Europe reaches back to the
same antiquity, none other combines with such
an undivided charm the associations of the past,
the interests of the present.   It is the one name
and place, which, being raised high above
all party struggles, all local jealousies, over
all causes and over all cases, ecclesiastical as
well as civil, is the supreme controlling spring
which binds together, in their widest sense, all
the forces of the State and all the forces of
the Church.   It is the one name and place
which, being beyond the reach of personal
ambition, beyond the need of private gain, has
the inestimable chance, of guiding, moulding,
elevating, the tastes, the customs, the morals
of the whole community.   It is the one institu-

tion, which, by the very nature of its existence, unites the abstract idea of country and of duty with the personal endearments of family life, of domestic love, of individual character. This is the bright side of that ancient and august possession, which has steadied the course of our onward progress, and given us peace in the midst of tumults, and freedom in the midst of order. It is because of the greatness of this possession, that we so fervently pray and hope that he who is its destined heir shall be worthy of his noble inheritance. He knows, and we know, that on him henceforth, as by a new consecration and confirmation, devolves the glorious task of devoting to his country's service that life which is in a special sense no longer his but ours, for which his country's prayers, his country's thanksgivings have been so earnestly offered. He knows, as few in like positions have known, the mighty power for good which has, within our own memory, been exercised in that lofty sphere by one who, from early manhood to his sudden and untimely end, wore 'the white

' flower of a blameless life,' unscathed and un-
spotted even in that 'fierce light which beats
' upon a throne.' He has learned by the experience of these eventful weeks, he has had borne
in upon him by thousands and tens of thousands
of voices, that 'of him to whom much has been
' given, of him shall much be required.' Hardly
ever, in the long course of our history, has so
heart-stirring a prospect been opened, of be-
ginning life afresh, of taking the lead in all that
is true and holy, just and good, of finding in the
hundred calls of duty a hundred openings for
the best and purest enjoyment, of strengthening
the relaxed fibre (if so be) of English morals, of
raising and purifying the homes of the poor and
the tone of every grade of English society, of
becoming by the sheer force of a stainless and
guileless life a terror, not to good works, but to
the evil.

Over the tomb of a famous Prince, who lies
buried in this Abbey, and whose first entrance
on a new career of goodness and usefulness began
from the moment when he stood by his father's

deathbed within these precincts, there is carved
the flaming beacon or cresset light, which, says
the ancient chronicler, 'he took for his badge,
' showing thereby that as his virtues and good
' parts had been formerly obscured, and lay as
' a dead coal waiting light to kindle it, . . .
' notwithstanding he being now come to his
' perfecter years and riper understanding, . . .
' his virtues should now shine forth as the light
' of a cresset, which is no ordinary light.'   Such
a kindling of such a beacon light, which shall
reach as far as the fame of this Thanksgiving
has penetrated—such may God grant to him
whom the nation hopes by its prayers to have
won back to itself for ever.   'Give, O give thy
' servant wisdom and knowledge, that he may
' go out and come in before this people . . . that
' is so great.'   'The Lord preserve his going out
' and his coming in, from this time forth for
' evermore.'

But if this be what we expect from the
Throne, let us ask ourselves what the Monarchy,
what the Empire, what the world expects from

us. It is the glory of England that if the welfare of the Prince is the welfare of the people, not less is the well-being of the people the only safeguard of the well-being of the Prince. It is not with us, as in some Eastern or despotic states, where the Royal House dwells apart, withdrawn from all the surrounding influences of the country or the age in which their lot is cast. The breath of public opinion, of good or evil example, in our mixed and varied society, rises upwards as much as it descends downwards.

It is in our power, in the power of the people of England, to drag down the Throne, even in spite of itself, to the level, if so be, of our own meanness, triviality, or self-indulgence, as it is, thank God, also in our power, by the purity of our homes, by the sincerity and the loftiness of our purposes, to create the atmosphere in which the Throne must become pure and lofty, because it cannot help receiving the influences which ascend to it from below and from around. We, by raising up a constant succession of just, upright, loyal, single-minded citizens, of enlightened and energetic teachers, of far-seeing and unselfish statesmen, form a body-guard around the Royal House of England, even as the statues and monuments of famous Englishmen in this Abbey stand like a guard of honour round the shrines which contain the dust of our Princes and our Kings. Any breach in that sacred line of honest English hearts, any failure of duty, of vigilance, or of faithfulness on our part lays open the way for the destroyer to come in and lay waste the innermost sanctuary of the State itself. Our prayers, our thanksgivings, if they are to last beyond the passing moment, must take the shape, not of idle flattery or fond endearments, but of stern requirements of duty both from others and from ourselves.

We justly look down with mingled indignation and contempt on the miserable outrage against the Gracious Majesty of these realms. We are accustomed to regard with scorn the handful of misguided men, who seek to win

popular favour by appeals to the prejudices,
the passions, and the ignorance of the people.
But let us remember that these are not the
only or the chief dangers against which the
Nation is bound to protect the Throne. If
there be, as there have been in other times and
in other countries, those who, hovering round
the footsteps of the great, either for their own
selfish ends, or from mere weakness and com-
plaisance, or from mere vanity of vanities,
strive to serve them by smoothing the path
to sin, by making a mock at goodness, by
hiding the unwelcome truth, or repeating the
welcome falsehood—if there be any who, under
the guise of friends, play the part of tempter
and evil counsellor, who lie in wait for every
occasion to flatter, to indulge, and to corrupt
—if there be any such anywhere, these, far
more than wild fanatics or the feeble parasites
of the multitude, these are the real traitors,
the real enemies of Sovereign, Prince, and people
all alike.

It is for the growth of such as these that we,

the nation of England, are, in great measure, re-
sponsible before God and man.   They are bone
of our bone and flesh of our flesh.   It is by our
levity, if so be, that characters such as these are
encouraged in their wretched folly, as it is by our
firmness that they are discouraged and cowed.
They come out when the moral atmosphere
has been made dark around them, 'wherein
' all the beasts of the forest creep forth for their
' prey.'   But 'when the sun ariseth,' when the
bright burning light of a sound public opinion
is brought to bear upon them, 'they get them-
' selves together and lay them down again in
' their dens.'

On these then, and such as these, whoso-
ever they be, men or women, high or low,
the Day of Thanksgiving is or ought to be a
Day of Doom.   Against these, and such as these,
the nation is called upon to echo the voice of
most just judgment that goes up from every
honest heart.   On these, if on any human being
whatever, Christian society, English society,
ought to place its deliberate ban, its unmistake-

able mark of righteous indignation. Whatever may have been before, yet now, if after
the experience of these never-to-be-forgotten
weeks and days—if, after this solemn recogni-
tion of the value of our great institutions, of
the incalculable importance of the character of
our rulers—if, after this, the nation relaxes its
hold on the high vocation, which has thus been
marked out, our last state shall indeed be
worse than our first. If, after this, any such
as I have described, shall be found, betraying,
misleading, ensnaring those whom by every
call, human and divine, they are bound to lead
into all good and keep from all evil, such, if
there be any such, deserve the contempt of
man and the vengeance of GOD, as amongst
the meanest, or the weakest, or the most de-
testable of mankind.

There is yet one more topic on which I would
dwell. In those ancient days of the Jewish
monarchy and Jewish people to which the text
belongs, it was customary, on solemn occasions

when, as we read, 'the King and the people
'made a covenant with each other and with
'God,' to erect some monument, some towering
pillar, some massive altar, as a permanent
witness to themselves and to the world, in order
that they and all might for ever be reminded
of what they had pledged themselves to do.
It was a just and natural safeguard. Human
emotions are so transitory that they need some
such external monument or form in which they
may be consolidated and fixed.   Such a monument we are asked now to erect—most suitable
to the occasion, most lasting in duration, most
significant to the eye and the mind of England
for all future time.

It is the restoration, the completion of the
great metropolitan Cathedral of St. Paul, that
witnessed the solemn service which we here this
day, in the sister Abbey of St. Peter, have also
met, in our humbler measure, to commemorate.
It is in accordance with the varying characteris-
tics of these two venerable and majestic Churches,
that, whilst the Abbey of Westminster is inter-

woven by a gradual, silent, continuous chain, as
by 'the links of natural piety,' with the even
tenor, the stately pageants, the silent depar-
tures of our country's rulers and heroes, St.
Paul's Cathedral derives its historical interest
from single stirring incidents,—from the sudden
and terrible vicissitudes of its own rise and fall,
from the thunders of the Reformation at its
pulpit cross. It has received the burst of national
exultation at the destruction of the Armada, the
victories of Blenheim and of Trafalgar. It has
mourned with a mourning people over the
graves of Nelson and Wellington—

Who is this that cometh like an honoured guest,
With a nation weeping, and breaking on my rest ?—
Mighty seaman, this was he, great by land as thou by sea.

It has rejoiced with the universal rejoicing at
the unexpected recovery of an aged Sovereign
at the close of the century that is past. It has
now rejoiced, yet again, with the still wider joy,
over the yet more wonderful restoration of the
youthful Prince. In the circles of that same
dome, round those same wide-embracing walls,

that witnessed the covenant, as it may well be
called, between the Heir of the Throne and his
future people, shall now be carried on that glorious work which the mighty architect of the
Cathedral was compelled to leave unfinished,
which its most venerable historian and illustrious divine laboured in vain to accomplish, but
which, when completed, shall make the great
Protestant Cathedral of England worthy to look
in the face the great Roman Basilica, of which it
is even now a noble rival,—worthy also of the
magnificent future which more and more seems
opening before it, as the centre of instruction and
edification to the thousands of worshippers,
week by week, assembled within its almost
illimitable space.

For such a completion as this the greatness of
the Imperial Thanksgiving demands the united
help of the British Empire. For such a completion as this, let every Englishman give, far and
near, according to his means. Let none think
they can give too much, let none think their
contributions too insignificant, to commemorate

a day in which they have all taken part—
towards a great work, a world-renowned edifice,
which ought to have been finished long ago,
which, so long as a National Church exists
amongst us, every Englishman may call his
own, from the Queen in her palace down to the
humblest peasant or the most remote Noncon-
formist, throughout the length and breadth of
the land.

And when, in after days, Prince and people
alike shall gaze with admiration on its vast
interior, bright with all the splendours which
art and wealth can bestow, as even now they
look from far on those sublime proportions
which rise above all the smoke and stir of this
bewildering multitudinous city—may he and we
be ever reminded of the solemn thoughts which
have now filled our hearts—may he and we be
always able to look back upon this week with
thankfulness and not with shame—may he and
we then behold in that august edifice a standing
memorial of good resolutions, not broken but
accomplished,—of noble hopes, not disappointed

but fulfilled, of splendid opportunities, not lost
but cherished to the utmost,—of generous devotion, on our part, to our Queen and country, not
wasted in party strife but spent in the common
good,—of love for God's holy Name, not shown
in futile and fierce disputes about trifles but in
the great causes of justice, charity, and truth.
May we all be able to say ten, twenty years
hence, with as much sincerity as now, ' I was
' glad when they said unto me, Let us go into
' the house of the Lord.'

LONDON: PRINTED BY
SPOTTISWOODE AND CO., NEW-STREET SQUARE
AND PARLIAMENT STREET

www.ingramcontent.com/pod-product-compliance
Lightning Source LLC
Chambersburg PA
CBHW020253090426
42735CB00010B/1912